Hypnotism, An Introduction

By Anny J. Slegten

Hypnotism, An Introduction
Anny Slegten
Published by
Kimberlite Publishing House
www.kimberlitePublishingHouse.com

©2019 by Anny Slegten   20250130
All Rights Reserved. Printed in the United States.

No part of this book may be reproduced, stored in or introduced into a retrieval system, or transmitted, in any form or by any means – electronic, mechanical, photocopying, recording or otherwise – without the prior written permission of the copyright owner.

The author of this book does not dispense medical advice or prescribe the use of any technique as a form of treatment for physical, emotional, mental, spiritual or medical problems without the advice of a physician, either directly or indirectly. The intent of the author is only to offer information of a general nature to help you in your quest for physical, mental, emotional and spiritual wellbeing.

In the event you use any of the information in this book for yourself, which is your right, the author and the publisher assume no responsibility for your actions.

ISBN: 978-1-7752489-4-1
School Coat of Arms designed by Boomer Stralak
Book cover and Kimberlite Logo designed by Marietta Miller
http://www.execugraphx.com

The Kimberlite-Diamond Connection

Kimberlite is a rock type that was first categorized over a 100 years ago based on descriptions of the diamond-bearing pipes of Kimberley, South Africa.

Kimberlites are the mechanism by which diamonds are brought to the surface.

Kimberlitic rocks are the most important primary source of diamonds and the main rock type in which significant diamond deposits have been found so far.

Anny is familiar with many rocks and minerals as her husband was raised around quarries, and later worked in several mines in Canada.

Therefore, it was natural for Anny to choose kimberlite as an analogy to the soul residing within our body – as a diamond within the kimberlite.

Welcome to

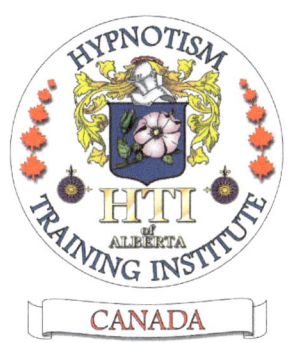

HYP 101—Hypnotism, an Introduction

This book belongs to

Name	_____
Mailing Address	_____
	_____
City or Town	_____
Province/State	_____ Postal Code/Zip _____
Country	_____
Telephone	Home (___) _____ Work (___) _____
Instructor's Name:	Anny Slegten
Today's Date:	_____

A course developed and updated
by
Anny Slegten
since 1984

All Rights Reserved.

*Our intention is
to offer a package
of simple, effective skills
that people can use
immediately
and every day
to better their lives.*

WARNING

The content of this seminar will make a profound impact on your life, for you will never again be able to say,

"I could not help it."

Sincerely,

Anny Slegten

This is what we intend to do:

1. Have a manual available to you to make it easier for you to stay focused on what you want to accomplish by taking this course.

2. Stay on target with specifics and examples.

3. Give you time to stretch your legs about every 90 minutes.

4. Have coffee, teas, and goodies ready for you.

5. Help you experience 6 different ways of going into a trance.

What you can do:

1. Participate - this is your course.

2. Have an open mind and be ready for some good laughter.

3. Tell us if you are not comfortable.

4. Complete your assignments.

5. Write down insights and ideas, also known as "ah-ha's" or mind grabbers.

Give a Man a Fish

- You feed him for one day.

Teach a Man How to Fish

- You feed him for a lifetime.

Living

versus

Surviving

"Getting By"

Being Accountable

versus

The Victim State

Describe the situation in your life that aggravates you the most:

_____

_____

_____

_____

_____

_____

Describe the *DISADVANTAGES* of your present situation and what you *RESENT* the most about your present situation:

_____

_____

_____

_____

_____

_____

Describe the situation transformed, as you would like the pleasure of experiencing it in the future (relating to what agrevates you the most) ...

Formulate the thought to the point of being able to write it down.

Be clear of your intent:

_____

_____

_____

On a scale from 1 to 10, with 10 being the highest, how successful have you been so far towards reaching that experience?

_____

_____

What knowledge do you want the pleasure of having by the end of this course?

_____

_____

_____

Please complete the following sentences:

I have wanted to be in charge of my life ever since ...
(describe what happened):

_____

_____

_____

This is what I have done so far to achieve that control ...

_____

_____

_____

So far, I have spent $ _____ in efforts to take charge of my life.

_____

_____

_____

This is what I have achieved so far …

_____

_____

_____

Please complete the following sentence:

I want to choose what happens in my life, to be in charge of my life, because ...

LIFE IS A CATALOGUE

You get

What you

Choose.

Regarding the situation in your life that aggravates you the most, describe the advantages and benefits of this situation and the advantages and benefits of your present limitations:

_____

_____

_____

_____

_____

_____

_____

_____

_____

_____

_____

_____

_____

HYP 101, Hypnosis, an Introduction

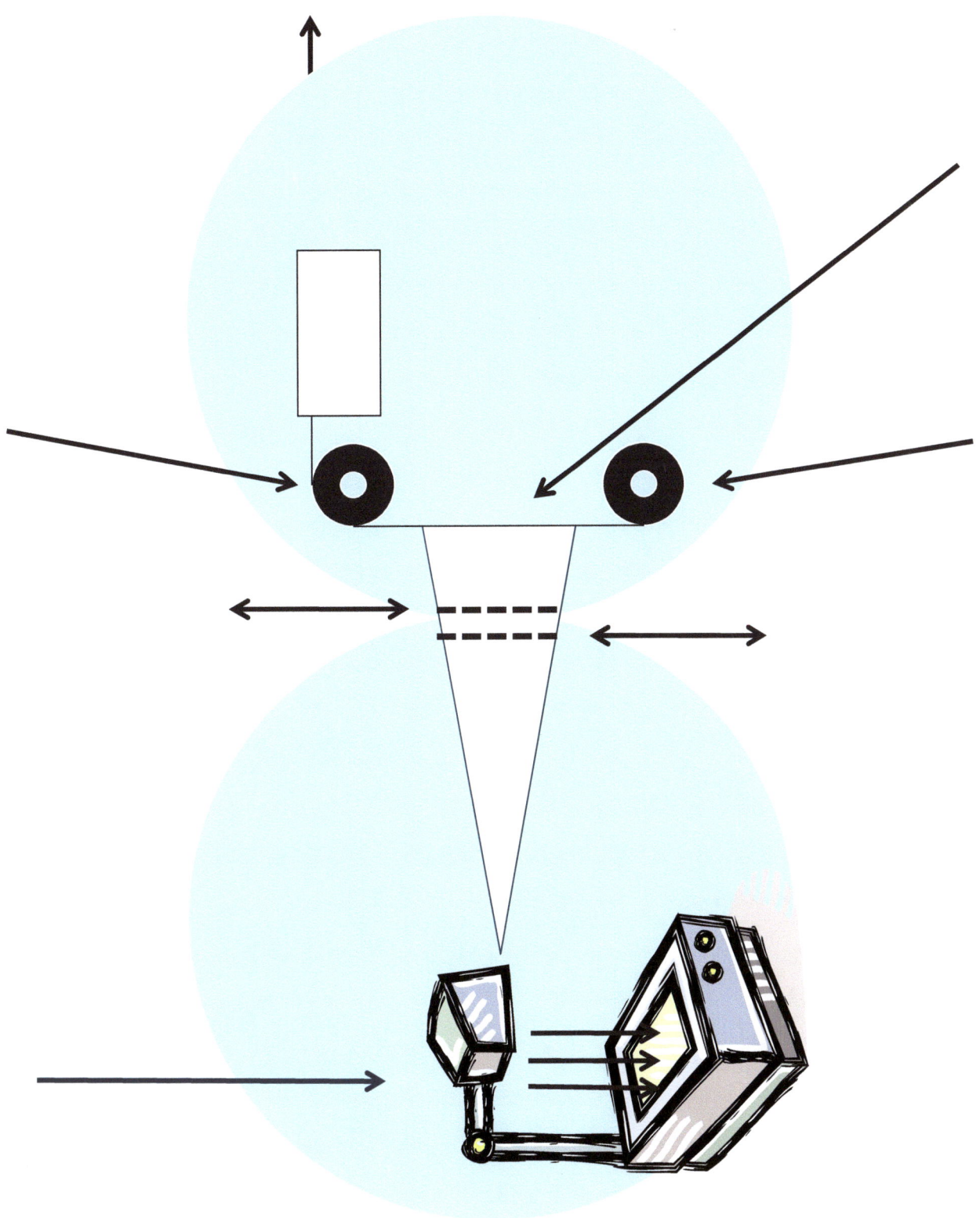

HYP 101, Hypnosis, an Introduction

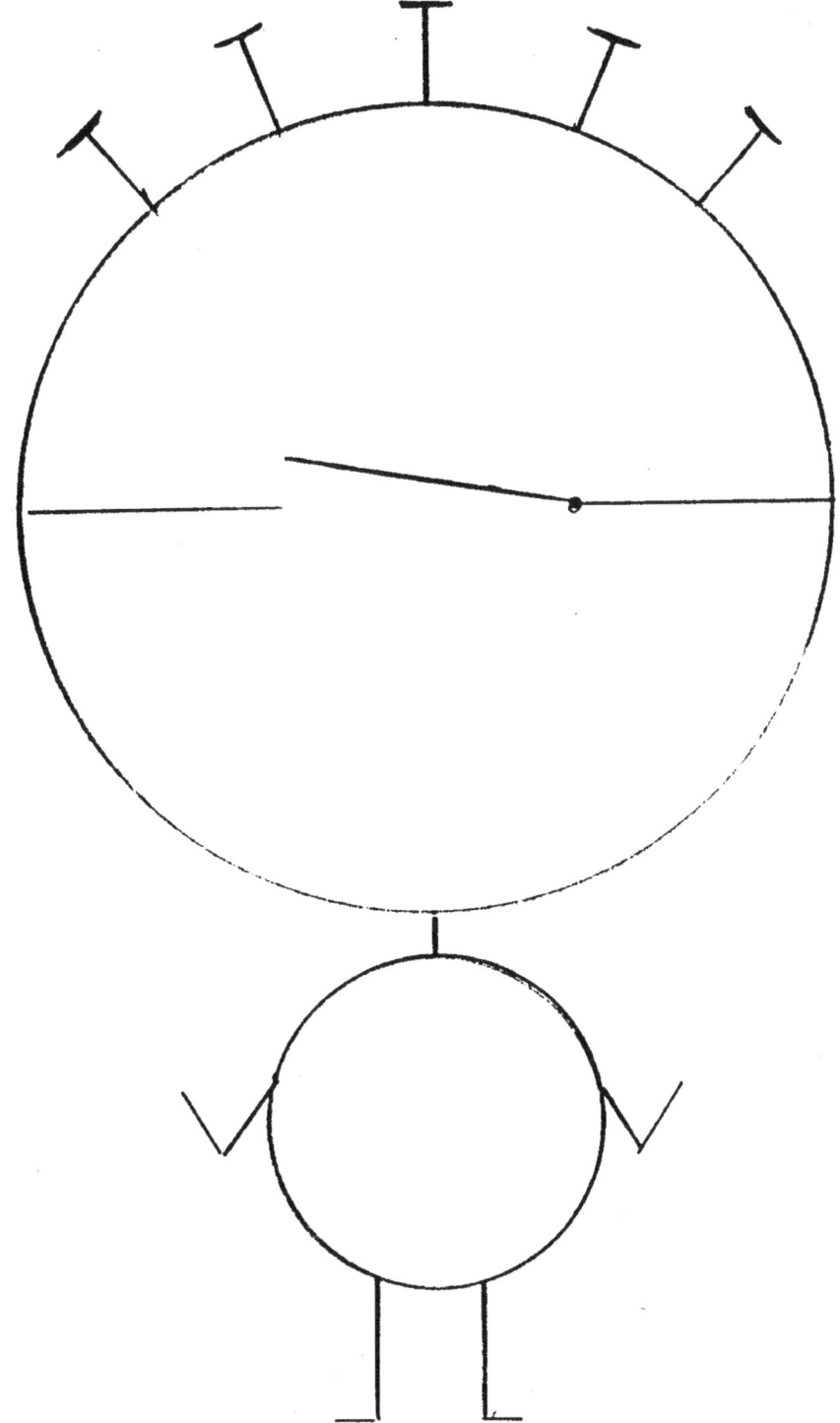

From Concept Therapy

INDUCTIVE and/or DEDUCTIVE REASON

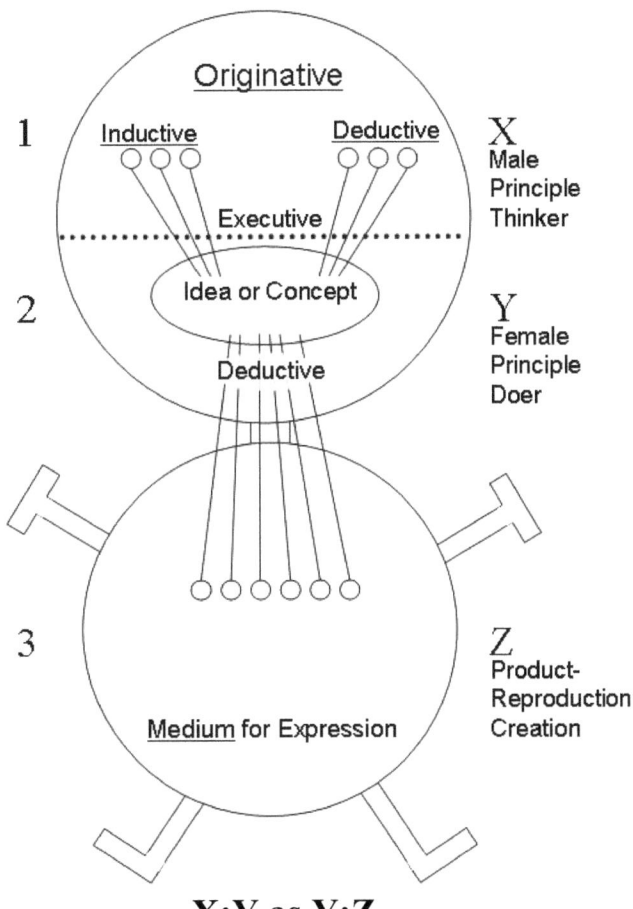

X:Y as Y:Z

Whatever X IMPRESSES upon Y,
then Y must EXPRESS in Z.

When an IDEA or SUGGESTION
is *logical* to the conscious mind,
it *lodges* in the subconscious; and
"when it lodges, you are hooked."

The expression in the body is interpreted as either
good or bad depending upon the nature
of the CONCEPT. Whatever IMAGE is
IMPRESSED upon the subconscious will
be brought into MANIFESTATION.

From Concept Therapy

Picture of what you concentrate on

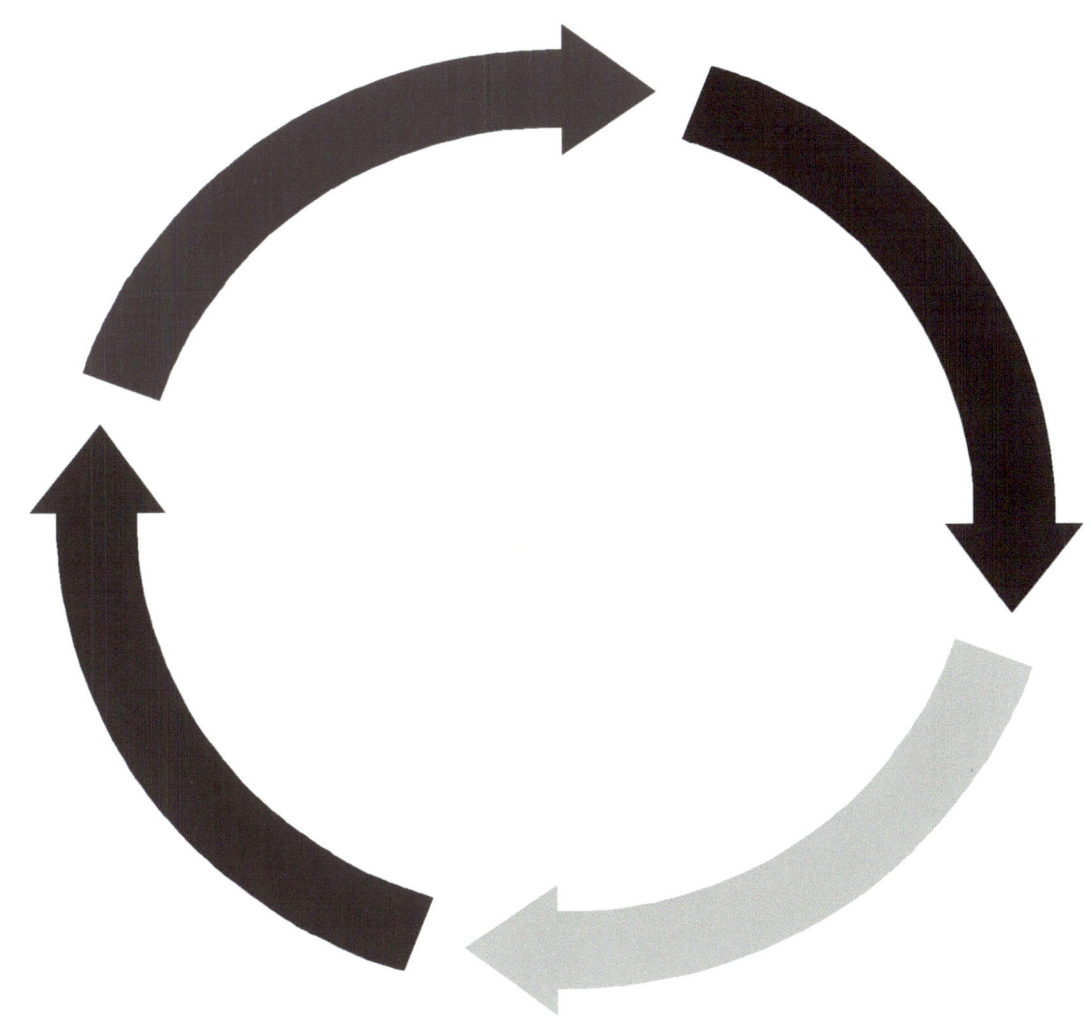

 Get what you concentrate on.

A thought creates a perception,
a vision that is impressed upon our subconscious mind by an emotion.

A thought, a knowing, creates a vision that is impressed
upon our psyche by the emotion it generates.

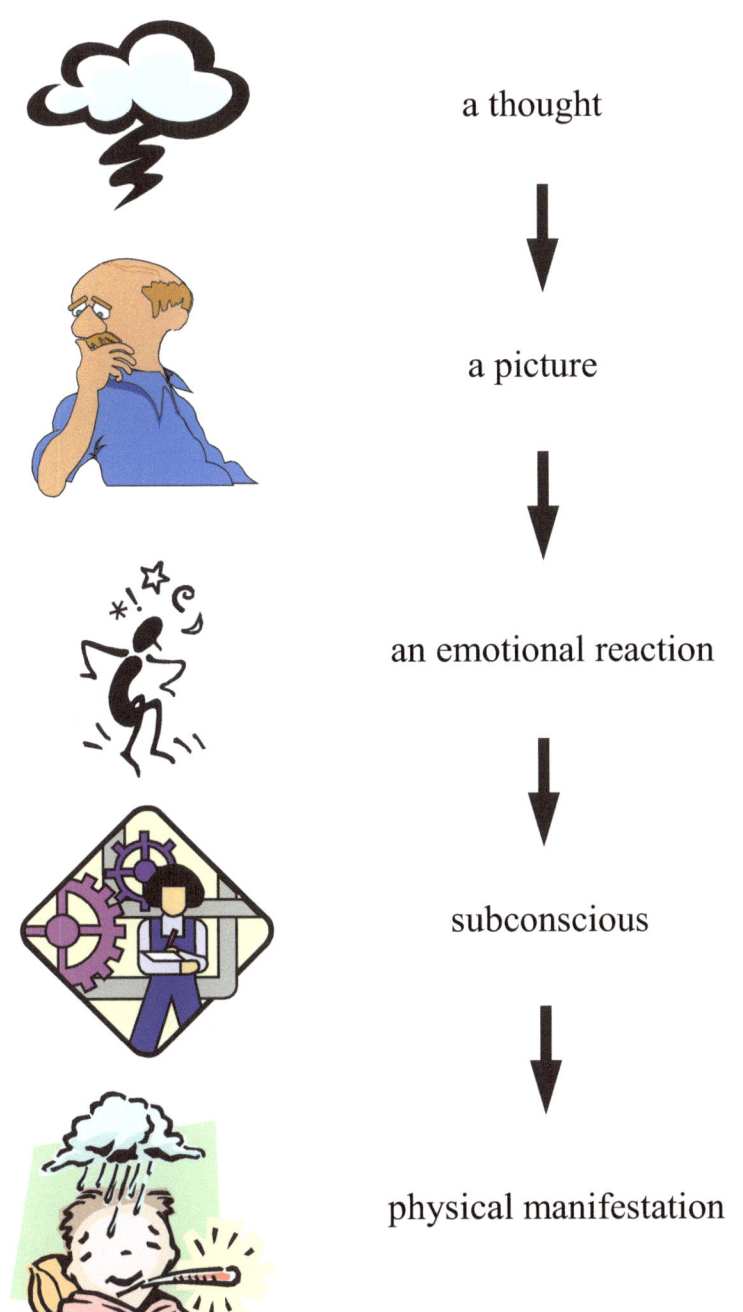

a thought

↓

a picture

↓

an emotional reaction

↓

subconscious

↓

physical manifestation

We are powerful entities
with the ability to create
our environment.

The creation is at subconscious level.

The subconscious mind is like fire:
a good servant and
a terrible master.

This is not Positive Thinking,
this is Positive Visualization.

HYPNOSIS

What is it?

How does it feel?

What does it do?

Anny Slegten   P.O. Box 3294, Sherwood Park, Alberta, T8H 2T2, Canada
Telephone 780.448.0817   Toll Free 1.800.330.5999. Facsimile .780.922.1147.   www.success-and-more.com

Trance - 1

Stare at a point on the ceiling overhead....

HYPNOSIS

A catchy word for:

- Altered State of Awareness
- Auto Suggestion
- Selective Awareness
- Altered State of Consciousness
- Mesmerism

Hypnosis is a moment of passivity
of the conscious mind
when the subconscious mind is

- allowed to *Express* itself

OR

- allowed to *Impress* itself

What is Hypnotizing or Programming?

It is a vivid picture, a vivid knowing impressed upon your subconscious mind by an emotion.

Live your picture, feelings and all.

When is your Subconscious Mind being influenced?

- When you are aware of it.

- When you are *not* aware of it.

When you are aware of it:

- Self-hypnosis

  _____

  _____

- Prayer

  _____

  _____

- Meditation

  _____

  _____

- Affirmation

  _____

  _____

- When hypnotized by a hypnotist / hypnotherapist

  _____

  _____

When you are not aware of it:

- by Violent Emotion

    - Happy _____

    _____

    - Angry (yelling) _____

    _____

    - Terrified _____

    _____

    - In a State of Shock _____

    _____

- by Fascination

    _____

- by Chanting

    _____

- by Falling asleep when devices are on: Eg: TV, Radio, Cell Phone etc…

    _____

- by Association

    _____

- by Inner Dialogue (Affirmation)

    _____

The subconscious mind is literal and will find the path of least resistance ...

Therefor always ask for THE PLEASURE OF ...

Affirmation

- Consciously

  _____
  _____
  _____
  _____
  _____

- Without Conscious Intent

  _____
  _____
  _____
  _____
  _____

Check your Language

- Words are more than what they sound like.

Check your Inner Dialogue

- This is your actual Programming.

What are you reviewing?

- You are reprogramming yourself,
  and reprogramming yourself,
  and reprogramming yourself,
  and .... etc.

Contemplate your Life

What you have now is what you were
focusing on yesterday.

What you have in your life today is
what you are giving importance to,
and keep reinforcing.

Solution

1. Be very clear at expressing your intent ...

   _____

   _____

   _____

2. Be aware of what you are telling yourself all day ...

   _____

   _____

   _____

3. Improve the way you are speaking to yourself ...

   _____

   _____

   _____

Demonstration on Experiencing our Beliefs

This story was published in the Sherwood Park and District Chamber of Commerce Newsletter in mid-1994.

The Man Who Sold Hot Dogs

There was a man who lived by the side of the road and he sold hot dogs. He was hard of hearing so he had no radio. He had trouble with his eyes so he read no newspapers, and he sold good hot dogs. He put up signs on the highway telling how good they were. He stood on the side of the road and cried, "Buy a hot dog!"

People bought and the profits were good. He increased his meat and bun orders. He bought a bigger stove to take care of his trade. He finally got his son home from college to help him.

But then, something happened. His son said, "Dad, haven't you been listening to the radio? Haven't you been reading the newspapers? There is a big recession. The European situation is terrible. The domestic situation is worse." Whereupon the father thought, "Well, my son has been to college, he reads the papers and listens to the radio, so he ought to know."

So the father cut down on his meat and bun order, took down his advertising signs, and no longer bothered to stand out on the highway to sell his hot dogs, and his sales fell almost overnight. "You are right, son," the father said to his boy, "We certainly are in the middle of a big recession."

Given by popular request -

The Prayer
Part of a Slegtenian Hypnosis Script as taught at
the Hypnotism Training Institute of Alberta

... and now, I am asking for your protection and well-being, and I say,

"God, please allow only good things to come to us, and for this blessing, we give thanks.

And now, you ask to be put into the protection of your Light, your very own Spark of Life. It is like a mini Sun in your chest. That light is the center of your being. That light is you!

Concentrate on it, and let it shine, let it shine! Let it shine throughout every cell of your body, throughout your aura, cleansing your body, cleansing your aura, extending itself at one arm's length above you, beneath you, on each side of you, in front of you, and behind you, and mentally repeat with me:

*"This is my body, this is my space,
only light can come to me,
only light can come from me,
only my light can be here."*

Given by popular request -

Coming out of Hypnosis
Part of a Slegtenian Hypnosis Script as taught at
the Hypnotism Training Institute of Alberta

* Note: Say the numbers outloud as your recite each paragraph.

Now I'm going to count from one to five, and then I'll say:

> *"Your eyes are open and you are fully aware. You are rested, refreshed, relaxed, and feel wonderfully good."*

One, Slowly, calmly, easily and gently beginning to return to full awareness once again.

Two, Each muscle and nerve in your body is loose, limp and relaxed, and you feel wonderfully good.

Three, From head to toe, you are feeling better in every way, physically better, mentally better, emotionally cool, calm, and serene.

Four, Your eyes begin to feel sparkling clear as if they were bathed in cool spring water.

Five, Eyelids open: you are fully aware. Take a good deep breath, fill up your lungs, open your eyes, and stretch.

Suggestion of some reading material giving information on what can be achieved with selective awareness (hypnotism)

Self Hypnotism
by Leslie M. LeCron
The many applications of hypnosis.

Super-Learning
by Sheila Ostrander and Lynn Schroeder
Selective awareness for learning.

The Secret Life of the Unborn Child
by Thomas Verny, M.D. with John Kelly
Age regression all the way to the womb.

The Power of Your Subconscious Mind
by Dr. Joseph Murphy
Good easy reading.

Past Lives, Future Lives
by Dr. Bruce Goldberg
The title says it all. Fascinating.

You Have Been Here Before
by Dr. Edith Fiore
A psychologist looks at past lives.

Getting Well Again
by O. Carl Simonton, M.D., Stephanie Matthews-Simonton, and James L. Creighton.
Your health and the power of your mind.

Professional Library

Traditional Hypnosis

Hypnotherapy - by Dave Elman

Naturalistic Hypnosis or Ericksonian Hypnosis

My Voice Will Go With You, The Teaching Tales of Milton H. Erickson - by Sidney Rosen

Uncommon Therapy, The Psychiatric techniques of Milton Erickson, M.D. - by Jay Haley

Neuro Linguistic Programming (N.L.P.)

Trance-Formation
Frog Into Princes
Reframing
 all by John Grinder and Richard Bandler

Using Your Brain for a Change
 by Richard Bandler

Spirit Releasement

Multiple Man, Exploration in Possession and Multiple Personality
 by Adam Crabtree

The Unquiet Dead, A Psychologist Treats Spirit Possession-Detecting and Removing Earthbound Spirit
 by Dr. Edith Fiore

Stories from the other Side
 by Anny Slegten
  Conversations with those who passed away, is an account of what happens when we physically die, as well as the Soul's journey and return to the Universal Energy Field. This book is available at Anny's office or at www.amazon.com

Homework

- Script for a motivational recording, A "Self-Talk" recording.

- A mental picture of you having reached your goal.

Be Precise!

Trance - 2

Focusing on a sound...
a song, an air conditioner, a humidifier, the sound of an airplane ...

Welcome to Day #2!

Today we will examining …

1. Consciously obtain the co-operation of the Subconscious Mind.

2. Sleep therapy.

3. Establishing rapport with babies and pets/animals.

4. Turning goals into reality.
   - Waking Hypnosis
   - Self-Hypnosis

1. What do you want out of this course?
   Present

   _____

   _____

   _____

2. What are you after?
   Future

   _____

   _____

   _____

3. On a scale of 1 to 10 (10 being the highest), how successful have you been at reaching what you are after at this point in time?

   _____

   _____

   _____

Is your life a journey? Or is your life a destination?

What is your goal?

_____

_____

_____

(In the last 12 months) To reach your goal, how many times have you:

- sought advice   _____
- taken courses and workshops   _____
- bought books, tapes, CDs   _____
- taken action   _____

On a scale of 1 to 10 (10 being the highest), how much did it help you?

_____

_____

What were the results?

_____

_____

_____

_____

_____

If you had reached your goal

What would be different in your life?

What would you do that you do not do now?

What would you have that you do not have now?

What would you be experiencing that you do not experience now?

_____

_____

_____

_____

_____

_____

_____

_____

_____

Trance - 3

Meeting Your Mental Picture
Write Down Your Experience

Trance - 3 Continued...

More Space To Write Down Your Experience

Resistance

What do you need?

_____

_____

_____

_____

_____

_____

What do you want the pleasure to have?

_____

_____

_____

_____

_____

_____

_____

... When I 'worry' about someone ...

I'm not believing in them,
I'm only giving myself power,
and they become weaker ...

... When I 'care' about someone ...

I'm believing in them,
and I'm giving them extra strength
to become stronger.

Source: Reflections for Living Life Fully
by Brock Tully

How Ideas Can Affect Organs and Glands

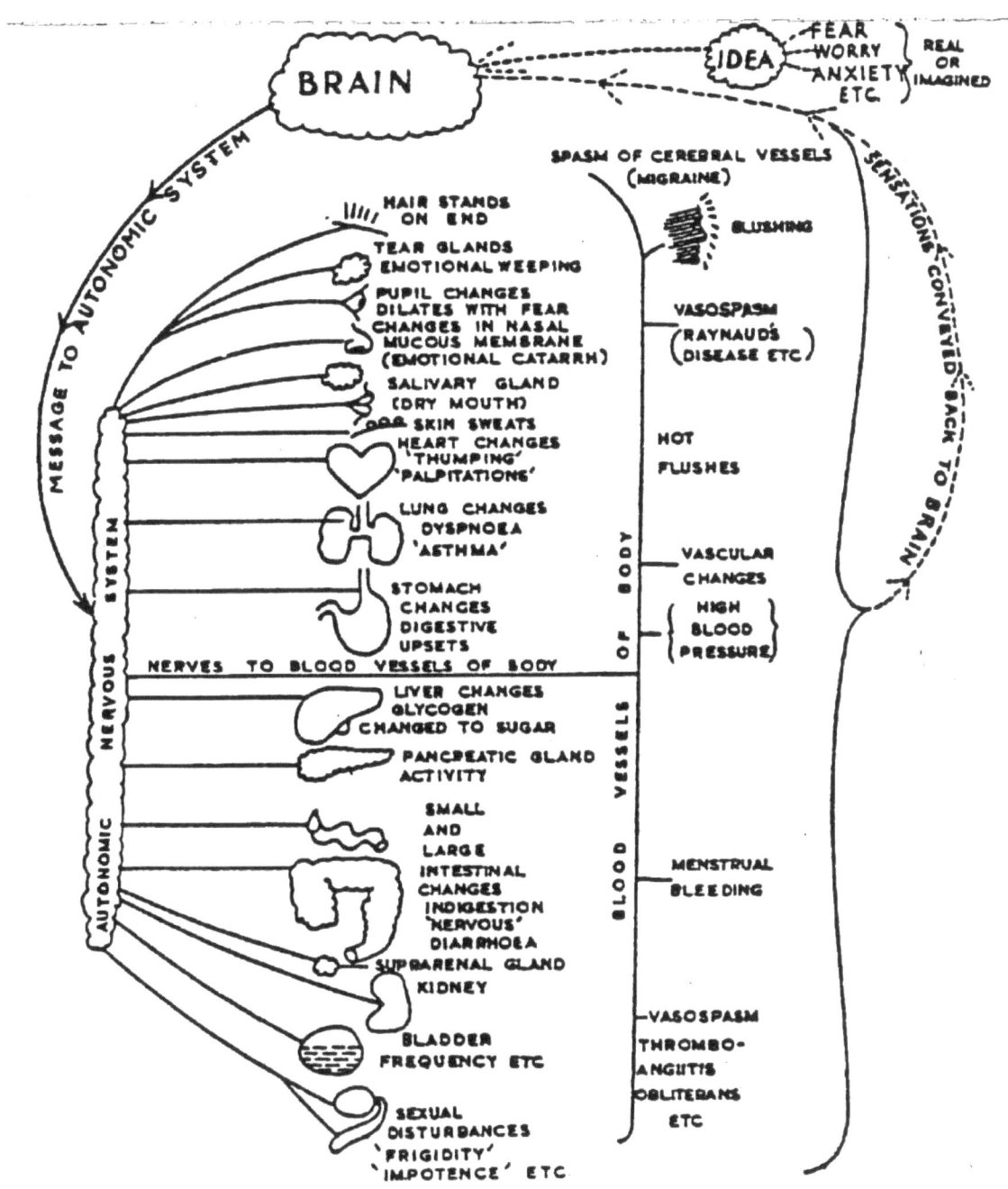

Purely diagrammatic sketch to show how ideas can affect body organs and cause changes via the autonomic nervous system.
(by courtesy of the British Journal of Medical Hypnotism)

How a Neurosis Develops

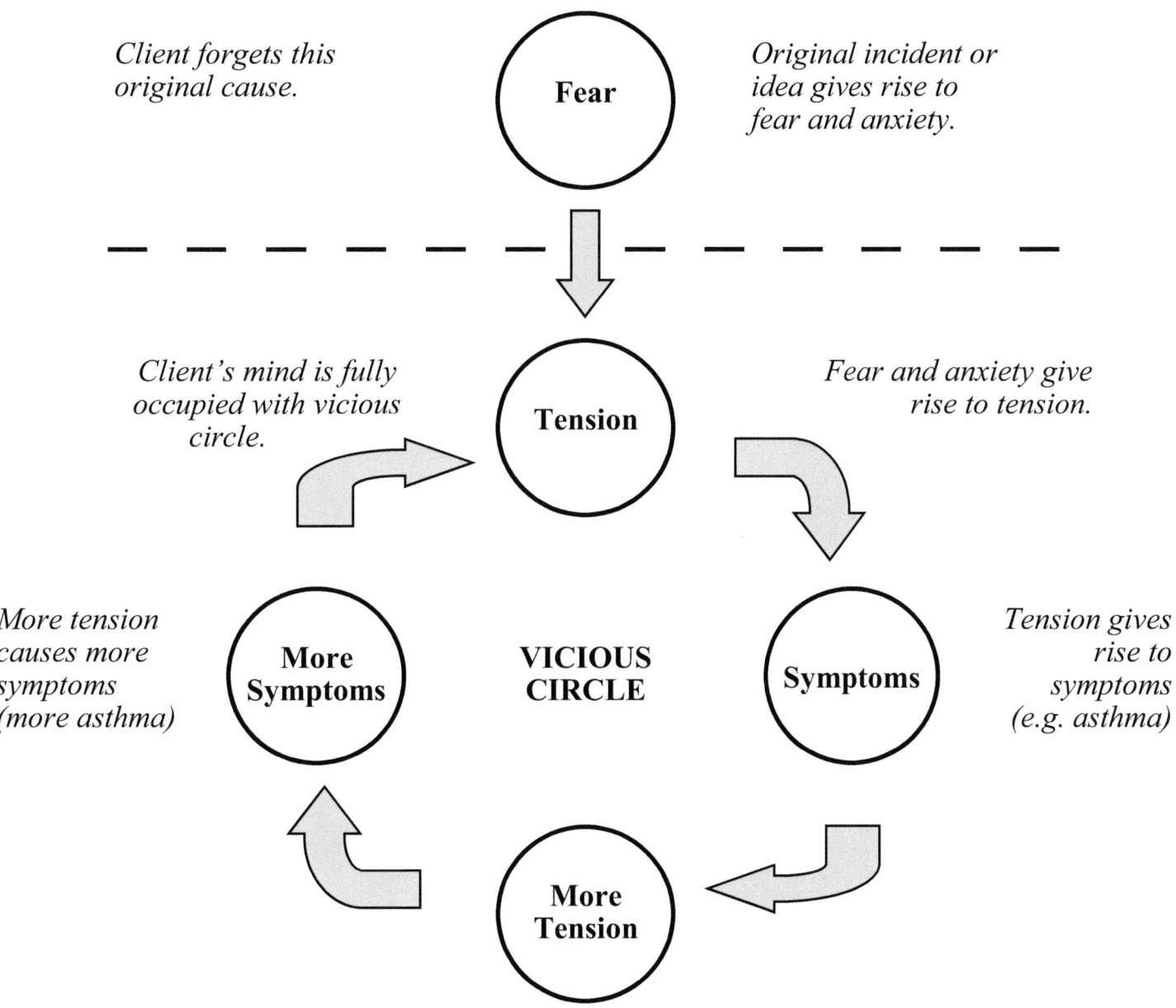

List of Elements of Emotional Ailment

- Conflicts

  _____

  _____

- Motivation

  _____

  _____

- Effects of Suggestion

  _____

  _____

- Organ Language

  _____

  _____

- Identification

  _____

  _____

- Self-Punishment

  _____

  _____

- Past Experiences

  _____

  _____

Examples of Messages from our Subconscious Mind

Mental Activities During Our Sleep

During the state of sleep, the conscious mind is turned off and we become easily aware of another part of ourselves. We have within us a link that connects us to the Universal Intelligence. That link, I call the subconscious mind.

The subconscious mind is the seat of great activity twenty-four hours a day. We usually are aware of it when we sleep.

Glimpses of the Past *(in this life or lives prior to this one)*
This can also happen during our waking hours. The information is usually clear and signals that we are subconsciously ready to reveal the situation to our consciousness.

Astral Projection *(also known as Out-of-Body Experience)*
To my understanding, it is one of the ways we stay sane. It is not easy for our Soul to stay confined into the body while remembering at a very deep level the freedom of being a Spirit.

One of the signs is all of a sudden "jumping" while laying in bed. This happens when we "reel ourselves back into our body" too fast! When we are ready to "lift up", we experience the delightful Astral Sway. It is believed we do Astral Projection from conception on.

A Near Death Experience happens when the body is dead. Astral Projection happens when the body is alive.

Clairvoyance and Clairaudience
When we are ready to fall asleep, there is a time when we are not asleep yet and we know we are not awake anymore, or when we are waking up, there is a time when we are not asleep anymore, and we know we are not awake yet.

During that in-between time we are in a very deep altered state of awareness (trance). It is then that we are most receptive to information about the future. It is almost like a complete movie of the future in front of us in a fraction of a second. It is also then that we receive precise inspirations and problem-solving ideas.

Dreams are always symbols
Since the information always comes in symbols, to understand them is the subject of many techniques. The information is always to the benefit of the dreamer.

Dreams:
Your Subconscious Mind Getting Your Conscious Attention

In a dream, our subconscious mind releases information using symbols, metaphors, making us wonder what the whole thing was all about! I have found it very interesting that the symbols in a dream usually have the same meaning as the symbols of the Tarot ... for example, the Devil represents our emotions; Death in the Tarot, just like in a dream, announces the end of a situation and a renewal, going forward, growth. The Death card is one of the best cards in the Tarot, so rejoice when you dream of your own death!

Dreams - What do you do with them?

- Wake up quickly
- Write down your dream, using the present tense
- Write down every detail of your dream
- Write down good and bad dreams
- Write down how you felt upon awakening from the dream.
- Have a Dream Journal; dreams have sequences. A story will unfold.

Since all techniques to understand the messages of the dream require that we go back into the dream, remembering how we felt upon awakening from the dream will facilitate this process.

Two of the many excellent books on the market are:

Lucid Dreaming, by Stephen LaBerge, PhD.

The Jungian-Senoi Dreamwork Manual, by Strephon Kaplan-Williams

To consciously impress our mind, we want to have:

1. The Desire

   _____

2. The Proper Mood

   _____

3. To Consciously Make a Picture

What your goal consists of:

- Do you really want it?

  _____

  _____

- Is there a conflict?

  _____

  _____

- Do you need someone else's co-operation?

  _____

  _____

- Is the goal expressed in a positive way?

  _____

  _____

When the Imagination
and the Will
are in Conflict,
the Imagination
Always Wins.

- Emile Coué

The language
of your
Subconscious Mind
is a
Picture

What is a vision?

It is the art of seeing the invisible.

Visions are memories yet to be experienced.

The simpler the understanding,
the more powerful the result.

The Applications

1. Know what you want the pleasure to have, experience and sustain.

2. "Mail" your request.

3. Go for it.

Cliches

_____

_____

_____

_____

_____

_____

_____

_____

Negativity is where the power is.

Acknowledging it - is very different from accepting it,
and usually defuses it.

Waking Hypnosis

Without conscious intent

- self-talk

- a thought

- words from songs

- caught up in emotions

With conscious intent

- motivational recordings

- affirmations

- conscious visualization

- creative activities

Example of "Waking" Hypnosis

As you start writing this letter to yourself, project yourself a year from now and pretend you are sending a letter to a friend, explaining what the past year has brought you. Use the present and/or past tense.

In that letter, describe the situations you projected. When you have finished writing the letter, fold it and put it in an envelope, and in your imagination, pretend you are including some photographs of yourself. The photos are confirming what you wrote in the letter.

Once a day, preferably in the morning,

1. Read your letter out loud.
2. Visualize, picture in your mind what you are reading.
3. Feel the satisfaction of having what you describe.
4. Put yourself in the picture.
5. Fold the letter and put it back into the envelope.
   As you are doing so, pretend putting the photographs of yourself in the envelope too, ready to be mailed.
6. Go on with your routine, "forgetting" the letter, having mentally mailed it - so to speak - letting it go.

There will come a time when, as you think of reading your letter out loud, in a fraction of a second you will "see" a vivid picture, the photographs so to speak, and this is really all that is required.

When you feel your mind is saturated by the "picture", let it go totally, knowing your subconscious mind *"Got the picture"*.

It is my experience that starting a new project with a new letter with new photos is the most effective way of letting go.

The "New Year Resolutions" Ritual
by Anny Slegten
Master Hypnotist,
Clinical Hypnotherapist.

Although I was raised in Congo (formerly Belgian), there is a tradition I faithfully follow from my native Belgium, namely "The New Year Resolutions" ritual. This is something I learned from my parents, both from Belgium.

As the New Year is getting closer, I review what the year about to draw to a close has given me and start to think of what I want the New Year to bring me, very similar to "what I want from Santa" here in Canada, except that this is a very precise list of what I want the New Year to give me over the next twelve months.

This is very much like the "Year End" ritual of a business! As the books are getting ready for the accountant, there is a review of how things went and an evaluation of the direction that was chosen previously. Then comes the new vision concerning where the business is to be by the next "Year End".

I am fascinated by the "New Year Resolutions" that are taking place. This is a time when people decide what they are going to deprive themselves of! Have you noticed? "Going on a diet," "Quitting smoking," "Stopping whatever," ... the list is long and varied. It is no wonder the resolutions are short-lived.

Through the years, I have discovered that life was not so great each time I did not take the time to make my "New Year Resolutions" list. It is like driving a car: when the vehicle is going into a skid, your car usually comes to a stop in the place you were focusing on. The "List of Wants" steadies the journey of daily life, putting us safely back on the road in spite of the "skids" we sometimes get ourselves into.

I take several weeks to do my list of what I want the New Year to bring me. As I review it prior to the final list, I am often finding that what I thought I wanted was quite different from what I really want. The New Year is a new beginning. Give yourself a chance; go ahead, make your list of wants. Just like in business, give your life a direction that you can look forward to. How surprised will you be to find out this type of "New Year Resolutions" actually works? Your life is your business, treat it as such.

Bonne Année a vous tous!

HYP 101: Self Hypnosis for Today's Living

Instructions for a Goal-Getting Audio Recording

Write down your goal, following the instructions you received during the workshop. Be very descriptive, including how you feel. Be precise, using the first, second, or third person (I want, you want, or he/she wants). Remember to mention "the pleasure of ..." often!

Where appropriate, add these sentences:

I (you, s/he) ask(s) my (your, his/her) subconscious mind, open and receptive to the suggestions it is receiving now, to sort all things out and heal, clear, and resolve whatever should be healed, cleared and resolved, so that I (you, s/he) can have the great pleasure of experiencing my (yours, his/her) wants in a most successful, diplomatic, and joyful way.

And the benefits of these suggestions whill stay with me (you, him/her) for hours, days, weeks, and years to come, much to my (your, his/her) surprise and delight. And for these blessings, I (you s/he) give(s) thanks.

And I (you, or s/he) ask(s) my (your, his/her) subconscious mind, open and receptive to the suggestions it is receiving now, that from now on, each time I (you, s/he) hear(s) the music used as background music for this recording, it will trigger the suggestions on this recording, much to my (your, his/her) surprise and delight.

Read the finished product several times aloud, to make sure it is what you really want. Do this for several days. This must feel right to you.

Once you are satisfied with the finished product, record yourself reading the script, using background music.

Make sure you have a recording of the background music by itself - so you can listen if you're in public and don't want others to hear the suggestions on your recording.

Play the recording when you are alone. When privacy is required, play the music only - your subconscious will automatically recite your goals for you.

Remember: Keep your goal(s) to yourself!

*If you can imagine it,
you can achieve it.*

*If you can dream it,
you can become it.*

- William Arthur Ward

---

*You can pretend anything,
and master it.*

- Milton Erickson

Practice it until you make it!

- Anny Slegten

Anny Slegten   P.O. Box 3294, Sherwood Park, Alberta, T8H 2T2, Canada
Telephone 780.448.0817   Toll Free 1.800.330.5999. Facsimile .780.922.1147.   www.success-and-more.com

Trance - 4
Practice For Relaxation

Eye Fatigue
Variation On A Theme

1. Ask the person for permission to help them relax.

2. If possible, put some soothing music on and ask the person to think about something pleasant and familiar. If wearing glasses, ask the person to remove them.

3. Instruct the person to:
   - stare at your fingers and follow them as you move them right up and down.
   - close their eyes as your fingers come down as the person exhales
   - to open their eyes again when they is ready.

Do this 3-4 times consecutively. Move your fingers in a slow vertical motion and observe their eyes for signs of relaxation. The eyes will probably water and redden.

If necessary, hold your fingers up a little longer to fatigue their eyes.

The prayer:

… and now, I am asking for your protection and well-being, and I say: "God, allow only good things to happen to us …

And for this blessing, we give thanks.

And now, become aware of your light. Your light, the spark of life that you have within you.

It is like a mini-Sun in your chest. That light is you!

Concentrate on that Light, and let it shine, let it shine! Let it shine throughout every cell of your body, throughout your aura, cleansing your body, cleansing your aura, extending itself at one arm's length above you, beneath you, in front of you, behind you, on each side of you, and mentally repeat with me:

"This my body, this is my space. Only light can come to me, only light can come from me. Only my light can be here."

And now, as I count down, find yourself going deeper and deeper with every breath that you take:

10, going down. 9. 8. 7. Deeper and deeper. 6. 5. 4. It feels so good. 3. 2. 1 relaxing more and more.

When you are relaxed like this, your mind and your body regulate themselves to good health. So relax, and allow it to be so.

PAUSE

Continued…

Now I'm going to count from one to five, and then I'll say:

> *"Your eyes are open and you are fully aware. You are rested, refreshed, relaxed, and feel wonderfully good."*

One,   Slowly, calmly, easily and gently beginning to return to full awareness once again.

Two,   Each muscle and nerve in your body is loose, limp and relaxed, and you feel wonderfully good.

Three, From head to toe, you are feeling better in every way, physically better, mentally better, emotionally cool, calm, and serene.

Four, Your eyes begin to feel sparkling clear as if they were bathed in cool spring water.

Five, Eyelids open: you are fully aware. Take a good deep breath, fill up your lungs, open your eyes, and stretch. You are rested, refreshed, relaxed, and feel wonderfully good…

** NOTE**

Should the person show emotions, it is important to let them be. Remember that *the biggest gift of all is to allow*. Simply stay silent and allow the person to work out whatever emotion came up.

How to use Self-Hypnosis

1. Put yourself into Hypnosis

   _____

   _____

2. Flash the vivid picture of YOU on the screen of your mind.

   _____

   _____

3. In your mind, role play that vivid picture - your vision
   BE THERE!

   _____

   _____

   _____

   _____

   _____

Trance - 5
Self-Hypnosis: A Tool for Self-Improvement

To monitor yourself, you can record these instructions.

1. Know what you want, your goal.

2. In your mind, have a vivid picture of the results. Pretend you are sending a close friend a picture of *you*, and the picture is self-explanatory: Yes, *you* made it! Make sure *you* are the center of the picture.

3. Put some music on at a comfortable volume. Soothing music.

4. Decide at what time you want to come back to full awareness, or put the alarm clock on.

5. Make yourself as comfortable as possible. Loosen clothing that binds you in any way, and remove your shoes if they are tight.

6. Take a deep breath. Exhale. *Close your eyes.*

    Take another deep breath. Exhale.

    Prayer (your option).

    And as you take another deep breath, exhale, and your eyes still closed, turn up your eyes as if you wanted to look through your third eye.

    And as you take another deep breath, and exhale, just relax, let every muscle go loose and relaxed as you go in a deep state of relaxation.

    And now, on the screen of your mind, project the self-explanatory picture, making sure *you are the center of the picture.*

    In your mind, role-play the picture. Be there. Notice your body movements. Notice your smile, the spark in your eyes. Feel the satisfaction of "having made it".

7. And now, take a very deep breath and exhale. Just let go, and let a feeling of satisfaction flow all over you. And the benefits of this exercise will stay with you for hours, days, weeks, months, and years to come. And for this blessing we give thanks. Your heart full of love.

Please note:

Since you know what you want to do at the time you take the deep breaths, your subconscious mind will switch on "automatic" and will do the complete exercise should you "fall asleep" during self-hypnosis.

WARNING:

Keep your goals, your visions to yourself.

_____

_____

_____

_____

_____

_____

_____

How to Block an Influence

**Self-Hypnosis
is a
mental exercise
to get what you want
in the physical.**

It is the materialization of a perception,
a knowing, an expectation created by
thoughts and sealed by an emotion.

The owners manual is within us,
and with hypnosis, we can
consciously access the information.

Anny Slegten

Trance - 6

Down the stairs… meeting a Reflection of Self

BRAIN WAVES INFORMATION

DELTA   Deep Sleep
0.5 to 3 cycles/seconds

THETA   Trance, drowsiness, or light sleep
4 to 8 cycles per second

ALPHA   Relaxed wakefulness or light sleep
8 to 14 cycles per second

BETA   Active everyday consciousness
14 to 35 cycles per second

Voltage between head and other parts of the body become more negative during physical activity, decline in sleep and reverse to positive under general anaesthesia.

It is a change in voltage.

Information from:
The Body Electric
By Roberts O. Becker, MD and Gary Selden

A Letter To Yourself

Project yourself a year from now, pretending you are writing a letter to a friend, explaining what the last 12 months brought you. Use the past or present tense.

At this point, I am asking you to **write a letter to yourself**, dating it a year from now.

When you are finished writing your letter, fold it, put it in the envelope I gave you, seal the envelope and write your own name and mailing address on it. Your letter will be mailed to you a year from now.

Suggested format:

Date _____ (one year from now)

Dear _____ (Your first name)

It has been a year since I took HYPNOSIS 101, Hypnotism, An Introduction and this is what happened since:

_____

_____

_____

_____

_____

_____

_____

_____

Love you,

_____ *(Your name)*

Online Store, Contact, and More…

You may contact Anny by visiting any of her websites and scroll down the home page to the contact information.

http://www.annyslegten.com
    Anny's private website and online store.

http://www.success-and-more.com
    To find the description of the many services offered, and more.

http://www.htialberta.com
    The Hypnotism Training Institute of Alberta including descriptions of hypnosis and hypnotherapy courses given.

http://www.reiki-canada.com
    About the Reiki Training Centre of Canada.

http://www.slegtenianhypnosis.com
    Although open to anyone interested in this fascinating hypnosis modality, this website information is for graduates of the Hypnotism Training Institute of Alberta.

http://www.connectwithanny.com
    This is the best place to keep up to date with Anny – including seeing all her latest books and how to order them on Amazon.

Other books by Anny Slegten

Reiki Training Centre of Canada
Class Material
http://www.reiki-canada.com

Anny Slegten   P.O. Box 3294, Sherwood Park, Alberta, T8H 2T2, Canada
Telephone 780.448.0817   Toll Free 1.800.330.5999. Facsimile .780.922.1147.   www.success-and-more.com

This book is a must read for Reiki Practitioners
regardless of their spiritual lineage
and could be of great benefit to Energy Healers
http://www.reiki-canada.com

Anny Slegten   P.O. Box 3294, Sherwood Park, Alberta, T8H 2T2, Canada
Telephone 780.448.0817   Toll Free 1.800.330.5999. Facsimile .780.922.1147.   www.success-and-more.com

The Many Ways of Reiki
http://www.reiki-canada.com

The Reiki Training Centre of Canada
Teacher's Manual
http://www.reiki-canada.com

Stories from The Other Side – Second Edition
http://www.connectwithanny.com

The Four Mental Agreements
To Losing Weight
http://www.connectwithanny.com

Anny Slegten   P.O. Box 3294, Sherwood Park, Alberta, T8H 2T2, Canada
Telephone 780.448.0817   Toll Free 1.800.330.5999. Facsimile .780.922.1147.   www.success-and-more.com

YOUR NOTES:

YOUR NOTES:

YOUR NOTES:

YOUR NOTES:

YOUR NOTES:

About The Author

As Director of The Hypnotism Training Institute of Alberta and The Reiki Training Centre of Canada, Anny has developed and structured the training and curriculum to the highest standards for both The Hypnotism Training Institute of Alberta and the Reiki Training Centre of Canada. She offers training to students that come from all over Canada and around the world.

Anny has experienced and lived in many corners of the globe and this has given her a unique understanding of many cultures.

Anny's Belgian parents were from the Flemish part of Belgium and were speaking Flemish (Dutch) at home. Living in Congo, everything was in

French.

Although she never spoke Flemish (Dutch), Anny speaks English with a guttural Dutch/German accent. Living in the English-speaking part of Canada for decades, Anny now speaks French with an English accent!

Anny is an Author and holds certifications as:

Master Hypnotist
Clinical Hypnotherapist
Hypno-Baby Birthing Facilitator and Instructor
HypnoBirthing^{TM} Fertility Therapist for Men & Women
Reiki Master/Teacher
Master Remote Viewer

Anny is a world renowned Clinical Hypnotherapist and Hypnologist in full time practice since 1984 as well as a Hypno-Energy worker since 2008.

In 1986 Anny created and developed an unique method using hypnosis for distance services - Virtual Sessions.

Over the years these Virtual Sessions proved to be an effective, useful, and efficient method for investigations and putting closure on both present and past issues - resulting in peace of mind.

To know more about Anny, please visit www.annyslegten.com and make sure to read what she published on her Blog.

Do you wonder what else Anny is publishing?

Visit http://www.connectwithanny.com

www.ingramcontent.com/pod-product-compliance
Lightning Source LLC
Chambersburg PA
CBHW060812010526
44117CB00002B/14